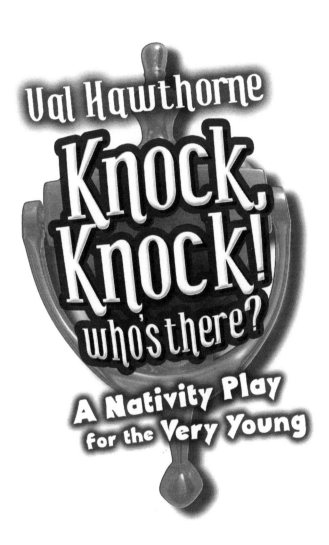

Val Hawthorne

Knock, Knock! who's there?

A Nativity Play for the Very Young

www.kevinmayhew.com

Public performance of this work is allowed only with permission
of the publisher and on condition that the appropriate performance
royalty is paid. Please refer to the licence form on page 63.
Further information about copyright will be found on page 4.

First published in Great Britain in 2013 by Kevin Mayhew Ltd
Buxhall, Stowmarket, Suffolk IP14 3BW
Tel: +44 (0) 1449 737978 Fax: +44 (0) 1449 737834
E-mail: info@kevinmayhew.com

www.kevinmayhew.com

9 8 7 6 5 4 3 2 1 0

ISBN 978 1 84867 646 6
ISMN M 57042 221 0
Catalogue No. 1450440

Cover design by Rob Mortonson
© Images used under licence from Shutterstock Inc.
Illustrations by Melody-Anne Lee

Edited by Donald Thomson

Printed and bound in Great Britain

Contents

A note about copyright in musicals

Copyright has existed for hundreds of years as a means of protecting the worth of a piece of music or text. It provides income for the author, composer and publisher and helps to keep the works available in print at an affordable price.

Performance licence

Any public performance of a piece of copyright music requires a licence. Music remains protected by copyright for 70 years after the death of the author or composer.

Even if you do not intend to charge an entrance fee for your performance, it is necessary to apply for a licence and the minimum fee will still be payable. If you are staging more than one performance without an admission charge, you need only pay the minimum licence fee once.

If you are charging for admission, the Performance Licence will cost 10% of gross ticket sales, plus VAT, subject to the minimum fee (see page 63).

The only time a performing fee is not payable is when the musical is performed within a worship service and forms part of the act of worship.

Photocopying licence

The words and music of the songs in our musicals are protected by copyright and may not be photocopied without permission. The music may not be photocopied at all – users are expected to purchase enough copies for those performers who require the full music. The texts may be copied for learning purposes only, provided that:

> The following acknowledgement is included on each copy:
> © **Kevin Mayhew Ltd.**
>
> **Used by permission from *Knock, knock! Who's there?***
>
> Licence number XXXX XXXX XXXX.
>
> You pay a copyright fee of £11.00 (inc. VAT), which should be added to your performance licence cheque (payable to Kevin Mayhew Ltd).
>
> All copies are destroyed after use.

Please note that music and texts of our musicals are not covered by a CCLI licence.

Duplicating CDs

Unfortunately we are unable to give permission for copying the accompanying CDs. It is illegal to duplicate any copyright sound recording, even for home use. If you have any queries about copyright in Kevin Mayhew publications, please call our Copyright Department on 01449 737978. There is a photocopiable licence application form at the back of our musicals.

Characters

2 Narrators

Postman

Mary

Joseph

Angel Gabriel

Donkey

3 or 4 Innkeepers

Shepherds – any number

Angels – any number

3 Wise Men

Pageboy(s) – depending on numbers

Someone to carry the star

Props

Door

Manger

Baby doll to represent Jesus

Postbag

Christmas cards

A large star on a long stick

Presents – Gold, Frankincense and Myrrh

Books for the Wise Men to look at

Projected picture of *The Light of the World*

Foreword

Knock, knock! Who's there? is a Nativity play for the very young with absolutely no rehearsals necessary!

Easy songs that everyone can sing, no difficult words to learn, something for everyone to enjoy and be involved in – this is what this simple Nativity play is about. It's an informal event for the very young in your church and for their friends and visitors.

You will need one or two 'up-front' adults to tell the story, interact with the children and encourage the congregation. It's quite good to have two people as a change of voice and style keeps people's attention. You will also need lots of costumes and plenty of willing helpers.

Some of your helpers will dress children and sort out who will be who. One or two will arrange the tableaux at the front as the story unfolds and there needs to be someone to guide children to the front as their turn comes. Try and sit all the dressed-up children together if possible. You may have young people in your youth groups who would like to be involved and could be a great help in all these jobs. Give everyone a script in advance so that they know what's happening.

You don't need to spend weeks practising in your Sunday School groups. The only thing that would be good is if your children could make some large Christmas cards to go in the postman's bag. You don't need to choose any characters in advance. Children can come along on the day, dress up and join in. Many of the big supermarkets these days sell Nativity costumes at very reasonable prices and I am sure you will have people willing to run up a few simple tabards and headwear for shepherds or angels. Gone are the days of dressing gowns and tea towels!

Most of the songs use tunes that everyone will know. There is one new song which is very easy to pick up. It would be good to have the words projected on a screen or alternatively printed on a programme. It is all very interactive with plenty to get everyone involved.

You will need a door! As you will guess from the title, there's quite a lot of knocking at a door so you do need to make some kind of door for children to come through. I know there will be someone in your congregation who will be only too happy to do this job!

This play had its first airing at Christmas 2012 in our church, St Jude's in Mapperley, Nottingham. A super door was made by one of our church members (it was supported by badminton posts) and we positioned one of our display boards at the side where children could 'hide' before they went through the door.

You will need a woodblock and someone to do the 'knock, knock' at regular intervals.

And one more thing – Christmas is a very special time. At the end of the play there is a message. Ideally you should have a picture of Holman Hunt's *Light of the World* displayed on your screen. If this is not possible try to have a copy to hold up.

While we have fun and we laugh and maybe shed a small tear as we watch the children, we remember that Jesus came to this world to be as one of us and to show God's love for us. We want to share this message because he is still here with us, knocking at our door, waiting to be let in.

VAL HAWTHORNE

About Val Hawthorne

A musician and former teacher, Val Hawthorne has worked with many children's choirs and school productions over the years as well as singing in and leading adult choirs and music groups. She is an active member of her local church and is very involved in its music and worship. Though retired from full-time work she keeps in contact with teachers and schools. Now, as composing has somehow taken over her life, Val likes to write lively, fun songs and plays that children will enjoy as well as thoughtful music with a Christian message. She also writes resources for church services. Any spare time is taken up with an increasing number of grandchildren!

Knock, knock! Who's there?

A Nativity play for the very young

As children arrive, greet them at the door and ask them if they would like to dress up. Allocate the various parts appropriately. When dressed, they can sit together near the front with one or two of your helpers. It doesn't matter if they prefer to sit with their parents.

The scene is set at the front of the church. Slightly to one side is the door with a screen at the side. In the centre is a chair for MARY. The manger and doll are somewhere hidden but handy.

Your woodblock player is ready. The knocking is highlighted in the script.

Position an adult behind the door to open it and guide children through.

The script is a guideline and need not be adhered to word for word.

Welcome

Have a jolly beginning. The leading adult could come down the aisle, perhaps in costume or at least with a bit of tinsel or headgear.

Greet everyone, with a special welcome to any visitors. Comment on all the children sitting dressed up. Give out any notices.

Start with something light-hearted, for example if two of you are leading, you could pretend that one hasn't turned up. Has (s)he got lost? Where can (s)he be? We can't start without him (her)!

KNOCK, KNOCK

Narrator 1 There must be someone at that door over there. Let's open it and see. . .

Enter the 'lost' person (NARRATOR 2). Have a little interaction.

Narrator 2 Hello everyone. I'm sorry I'm late. I'm so excited. I've been putting up decorations – wrapping presents – getting the turkey ready . . .

Narrator 1 Well you're here now. It is exciting on Christmas Eve *(or just before Christmas)* isn't it? Who feels excited? And I wonder if any of you are having visitors? Maybe some of your family are coming for Christmas dinner? Or perhaps you've got people coming for a sleepover.

Narrator 2   Visitors come knocking at the door, don't they? I think we might be having some visitors today who'll come knocking at this door.

KNOCK, KNOCK

Narrator 2   In fact, there's someone knocking right now!

Someone from your church can come through – your vicar or curate, a new member who is happy to be interviewed briefly or a very long-standing member. Have a short chat, ending with:

'Visitor'   I'm really looking forward to hearing the Christmas story again this afternoon. I can see lots of you are dressed up, ready to help tell the story. Are we going to start with a carol?

Narrator 1   We are. We're all going to stand and sing *O little town of Bethlehem.*

1. O little town of Bethlehem

CD Track 1

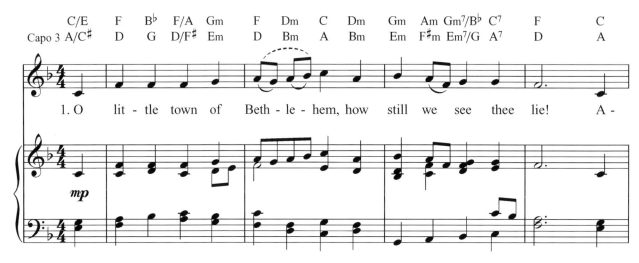

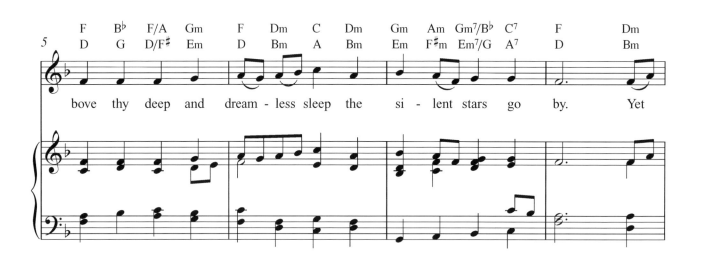

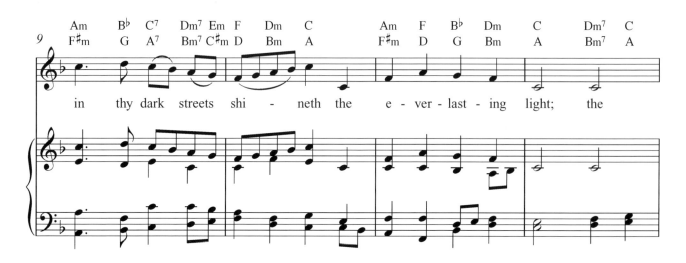

This music arrangement © Copyright Oxford University Press.
Used by permission from 'The English Hymnal'.

hopes and fears of all the years are met in thee to - night.

Words: Phillips Brooks (1835-1893) alt.
Music: Traditional English melody collected
and arr. Ralph Vaughan Williams (1872-1958)

2. O morning stars, together
    proclaim the holy birth,
    and praises sing to God the King,
    and peace to all the earth.
    For Christ is born of Mary;
    and, gathered all above,
    while mortals sleep, the angels keep
    their watch of wond'ring love;

3. How silently, how silently,
    the wondrous gift is giv'n!
    So God imparts to human hearts
    the blessings of his heav'n.
    No ear may hear his coming;
    but in this world of sin,
    where meek souls will receive him, still
    the dear Christ enters in.

4. O holy child of Bethlehem,
    descend to us, we pray;
    cast out our sin, and enter in,
    be born in us today.
    We hear the Christmas angels
    the great glad tidings tell:
    O come to us, abide with us,
    our Lord Emmanuel.

Narrator 1   Now everyone, when we hear a knock at the door
we're all going to say 'Who's there?'
Let's practise.

KNOCK, KNOCK

Everyone   Who's there?

Practise this once or twice more.

Narrator 2   And we've got a song about knocking at the door.
It's very easy. Listen first and then join in.

*During the song the postman gets ready behind the
screen. Play the CD or sing the song, to get everyone
ready to sing along.*

2. Who's that knocking at the door?

CD Track 2

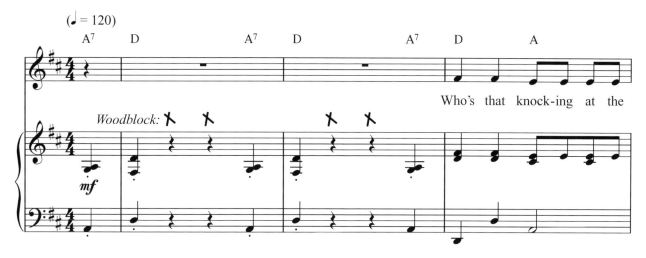

Who's that knock-ing at the

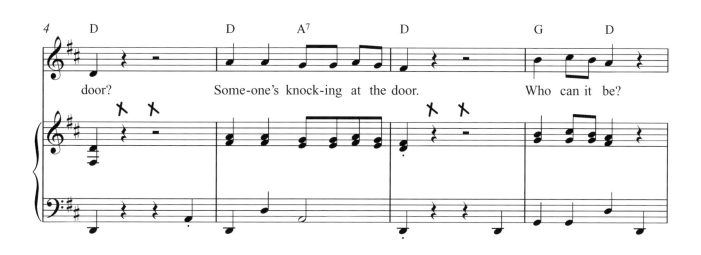

door? Some-one's knock-ing at the door. Who can it be?

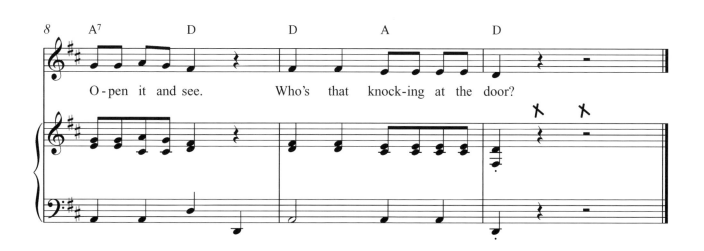

O-pen it and see. Who's that knock-ing at the door?

© Copyright 2013 Kevin Mayhew Ltd.
It it illegal to photocopy music.

Narrator 2   I think there might be someone coming now. Listen.

KNOCK, KNOCK

All   Who's there?

POSTMAN comes through the door (child or adult) with a postbag.

Narrator 1   It's the postman. Hello postman!

Postman   Hello!

Narrator 2   Have you got some post for us?

Postman   I have, in my bag here. *(If your postman is a child, he needs only nod and take out the cards.)*

Narrator 1   Maybe some children could help you.

POSTMAN goes to children near the front and lets them take a card out of his bag.

Narrator 2   Let's have a look. Christmas cards! I love receiving Christmas cards. These are lovely . . . a Christmas tree, an angel, a star and here's the stable. We'll put them over here where we can all see them. Thank you, postman. I expect you're very busy with last-minute deliveries.

Postman   I'd better be off now. Bye, everyone! Have a lovely Christmas.

POSTMAN walks off down the aisle, waving as he goes.

Narrator 1   Some of these cards tell the Christmas story. We're going to meet some more visitors in a minute as we tell the story together.

Let's sing the song again.

Repeat Song 2 (see page 13). During the song MARY, ANGEL GABRIEL and JOSEPH go behind the screen.

KNOCK, KNOCK

All   Who's there?

MARY comes through the door.

Narrator 1   Look. It's Mary. Hello Mary.
Have you been busy today? I think it's time for you
to have a sit down and a rest.

Repeat Song 2 (see page 13).

KNOCK, KNOCK

All   Who's there?

ANGEL GABRIEL comes through the door.

Narrator   It's an angel! This is Angel Gabriel who has come
to tell Mary something very important. He has
brought special news that has been sent from God.
We'll sing about it. You'll all know the tune.

3. Mary, this is special news

Tune: 'Here we go round the mulberry bush'

CD Track 3

1. Ma - ry, this is spe - cial news, spe - cial news, spe - cial news.
2. You will have a ba - by boy, ba - by boy, ba - by boy.
3. Je - sus is his spe - cial name, spe - cial name, spe - cial name.

Ma - ry, this is spe - cial news, sent from God in hea - ven.
You will have a ba - by boy, sent from God in hea - ven.
Je - sus is his spe - cial name, sent from God in hea - ven.

See page 46 for an alternative song: 'Mary, Mary, here comes an angel'

Exit ANGEL GABRIEL.

Narrator 2 Mary is surprised but she feels happy too when she knows that she is going to have God's baby son. I think I can hear someone else coming.

Repeat Song 2 (see page 13).

KNOCK, KNOCK

All Who's there?

JOSEPH comes through the door.

Narrator 1 It's Joseph. Mary is going to marry Joseph. Hello, Joseph. Have you come to see Mary? She has some exciting news to tell you. She's going to have a baby boy, God's son. His name will be Jesus.

Narrator 2 Joseph has some news too. Soon they will have to go on a journey to Bethlehem to have their names written down. Everyone in the whole country is being counted and they all have to go to the town where they were born.

Narrator 1 It's time now for Mary and Joseph to set off on their journey to Bethlehem. It's a long way, so they're setting off early. Mary will have to ride on a donkey.

DONKEY comes through the door.

Narrator 1 Here's the donkey. He can carry some of the luggage too. Off they go. Let's all wave them goodbye. Goodbye, Mary. Goodbye, Joseph. Safe journey.

MARY, JOSEPH and DONKEY walk around the church.

Narrator 2 We'll all sing as they go.

4. Little donkey

During the song, the INNKEEPERS get ready behind the screen.
The manger is positioned in the centre near Mary's chair.

CD Track 4

Lit-tle don - key, lit-tle don - key, on the dus - ty road,

got to keep on plod-ding on - wards, with your pre - cious load.

Been a long time, lit-tle don - key, through the win - ter's night;

Words and Music: Eric Boswell (1921-2009)

See page 47 for an alternative song: 'Joseph's song'

Narrator 1	Here they are in Bethlehem at last. It's very busy. Mary is very tired and it's nearly time for her to have her baby. They need to find somewhere to stay. I think they'd better try knocking on some doors.

Repeat Song 2 (see page 13).

MARY and JOSEPH walk up to the door.

KNOCK, KNOCK

All	Who's there?

The door opens and INNKEEPER 1 is standing there.

Narrator 2	Hello, Innkeeper. This is Mary and Joseph. They want to know if there is a room where they can stay the night.

If they want to speak, they can (see below), otherwise the INNKEEPER shakes his head and closes the door.

(Joseph	Please may we stay the night?
Innkeeper 1	Sorry. No room.)
Narrator 2	You'd better try somewhere else, Joseph.

MARY and JOSEPH walk around, then come back to the door and knock.

KNOCK, KNOCK

All	Who's there?

The door opens and INNKEEPER 2 is standing there.

Narrator 1	Hello, Innkeeper. This is Mary and Joseph. They've come a long way and would like to know if you have a room where they can stay.

INNKEEPER shakes his head and closes the door.

Narrator 1	Oh dear. You'll have to try somewhere else.

They walk around and come back to the door.

KNOCK, KNOCK

All	Who's there?

Narrator 1   Hello, Innkeeper. This is Mary and Joseph.
They *really* need somewhere to stay. Poor Mary is
going to have a baby soon. Have you got a room
anywhere?

Oh – this Innkeeper is nodding.
Look, he's beckoning. He says there's no room in
the house but he has a stable you can stay in.

Thank you, Innkeeper.

MARY and JOSEPH move to stable in the centre.

Narrator 2   Mary and Joseph settle down for the night.
It's warm and dry in the stable.
Some animals sleep there too.

It's very quiet. Outside the stars are shining.
Something very special is going to happen tonight.
A bright star is shining over the stable.

We'll sing a quiet song. We all know this song,
but instead of Twinkle, twinkle, little star we'll sing
Twinkle, twinkle, *special* star.

5. Twinkle, twinkle, special star

CD Track 5

Narrator 1   That night Mary's baby was born. She wrapped him up to keep him warm and laid him down to sleep on the soft hay in the manger.

Put BABY JESUS in the manger.

Narrator 1   We'll sing our song again like a lullaby.
We don't want to wake the baby.

Repeat Song 5 (see page 23), then repeat Song 2 (see page 13).

SHEPHERDS get ready behind screen.

KNOCK, KNOCK

All   Who's there?

All the SHEPHERDS come through the door.

Narrator 1   It's a lot of shepherds. Hello, shepherds.
Are you off to the hills to look after your sheep?
We'll all stand and sing as the shepherds go to the fields.

SHEPHERDS go and sit in the centre of the aisle.

6. While shepherds watched

CD Track 6

Words: Nahum Tate (1652-1715)
Music: from Este's 'Psalter' (1592)

See page 50 for an alternative song: 'See him lying on a bed of straw'

2. 'Fear not,' said he, (for mighty dread
   had seized their troubled mind)
   'glad tidings of great joy I bring
   to you and all mankind.

3. To you in David's town this day
   is born of David's line
   a Saviour, who is Christ the Lord;
   and this shall be the sign:

4. The heav'nly babe you there shall find
   to human view displayed,
   all meanly wrapped in swathing bands,
   and in a manger laid.'

5. Thus spake the seraph, and forthwith
   appeared a shining throng
   of angels praising God, who thus
   addressed their joyful song:

6. 'All glory be to God on high,
   and on the earth be peace,
   goodwill henceforth from heav'n to all
   begin and never cease.'

During the carol, the ANGEL GABRIEL and all the angels get ready.
The CHILD holding the star goes to stand near the stable.

Narrator 1 The shepherds are sitting round a fire to keep warm. Some of them fall asleep. But look! Suddenly there's a bright light in the sky. Who's going to come through the door now?

KNOCK, KNOCK

All Who's there?

ANGEL GABRIEL comes through the door and goes to stand near the shepherds.

Narrator 1 It's the Angel Gabriel again.
He's going to talk to the shepherds.

Let's listen to what the angel is saying.

NARRATOR 2 speaks over the background music 'Starry night' (see page 28).

Narrator 2 Shepherds, don't be scared, I bring good news,
a baby is born.
This is happy news for everyone,
a baby is born.

On this shiny bright, starry night,
a baby is born.
In the little town of Bethlehem
a baby boy is born.

In a cattle shed, a manger bed,
a baby's asleep.
So come and see, follow me,
find the baby asleep.

7. Starry night

CD Track 7

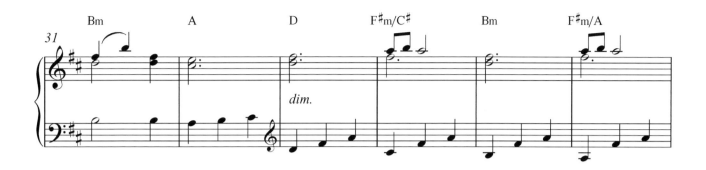

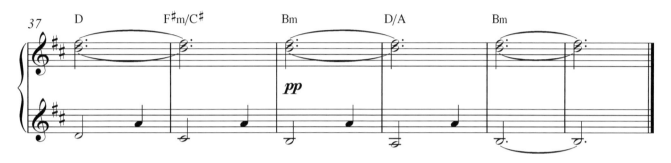

See page 48 for an alternative song: 'Shepherds in the fields one night'

Narrator 1 What exciting news! The shepherds can't wait to see the baby. But wait a minute. I think there's more knocking at the door.

KNOCK, KNOCK

All Who's there?

All the ANGELS come through the door.

Narrator 1 More angels! They're singing and dancing because it's such good news! We'll all join in.

8. Jesus is born in Bethlehem

Tune: 'The Hokey-Cokey'

CD Track 8

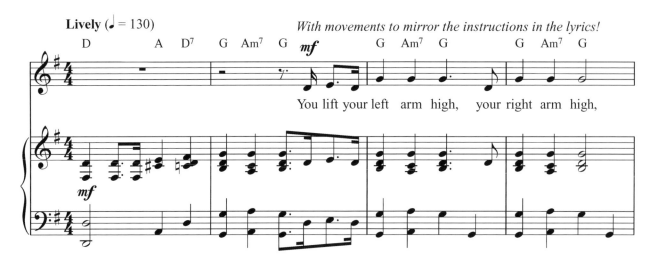

With movements to mirror the instructions in the lyrics!

You lift your left arm high, your right arm high,

left arm, right arm, wave them in the sky. You clap your hands to-ge-ther and you

turn a - round; Je - sus is born in Beth - le - hem.

During the song the WISE MEN and any PAGEBOYS get ready behind the screen.
After the song ANGELS go to stand behind MARY and JOSEPH.

Narrator 1 Off you go to the stable, shepherds.
There – you can see the baby Jesus.

Repeat Song 2 (see page 13).

KNOCK, KNOCK

All Who's there?

*WISE MEN and PAGEBOYS come through the door.
They can hold a book each.*

Narrator 2 Here are three very Wise Men. They're busy reading
their books. They've been outside looking at the
stars. They're pointing to the sky. There's a very big,
bright star they've not seen before.

The books tell them that it means a baby King has
been born – a King for the whole world. We know
about him, don't we? What's his name?

Yes, it's Jesus. Where is he born? Yes, in Bethlehem.
The Wise Men had better go and look for him.
The star will lead the way and we'll sing as they go.

*Take the books from the WISE MEN and give them
their gifts to carry.*

*The STAR comes and leads the WISE MEN and
PAGEBOYS as they walk up and down the aisle.*

9. Three Wise Men

Tune: 'Three blind mice'

CD Track 9

Rather heavy and plodding (♩. = 75)

Three Wise Men, three Wise Men

see a bright star, see a bright star.

Lead - ing on - ward to Beth - le - hem, shin - ing there o - ver Beth - le - hem;

fol - low the star up to Beth - le - hem, three Wise Men.

dim. al fine

See page 49 for an alternative song: 'Who is coming?'

Narrator 1 Here they are in Bethlehem at last. They've found the place where Mary and Joseph and the Baby Jesus are.

WISE MEN, PAGEBOYS and STAR join the tableau.

Narrator 2 They've brought some beautiful and very precious presents for the baby.

The first Wise Man has brought some gold because the baby will be a king.

The second Wise Man has brought some frankincense because the baby has come from God.

The third Wise Man has brought some myrrh because the baby will love us.

Narrator 1 I wonder if there will be any more visitors to see the Baby Jesus? I think all you children who haven't come up here already would like to see him. We'll all knock at the door. And after we've said 'Who's there?' everybody say your own name.

KNOCK, KNOCK

All Who's there? *(Everyone says their names.)*

Narrator 1 You can all come to the front to see the baby
and we'll sing 'Away in a manger'.

*All CHILDREN come to the front and sit round the
manger.*

10. Away in a manger

CD Track 10

Words and Music: William James Kirkpatrick (1838-1921)
arr. John Rombaut

2. The cattle are lowing, the baby awakes,
   but little Lord Jesus, no crying he makes.
   I love thee, Lord Jesus! Look down from the sky,
   and stay by my side until morning is nigh.

3. Be near me, Lord Jesus; I ask thee to stay
   close by me for ever, and love me, I pray.
   Bless all the dear children in thy tender care,
   and fit us for heaven, to live with thee there.

Narrator 1   We give presents at Christmas to remember that God gave us all a present. He gave us his Son Jesus to come and be with us and show us how much he loves us.

Picture of Holman Hunt's painting 'The Light of the World' appears on screen.

Narrator 2   This is a very famous painting. Look, you can see there's a door and someone knocking at it. The 'someone' is Jesus. Jesus didn't stay a baby – he grew up like all babies do. So here he is standing knocking at a door. And it's your door he's knocking at – the door of your home, the door of your life, the door of your heart.

If you look carefully you'll see there's no handle on the door. That's because it's inside and you have to open it to let Jesus in.

He would love to come in and be your friend.

There's a verse in the Bible that says: Here I am. I stand at the door and knock. If anyone hears my voice and opens the door, I will come in.

Let's open our door for Jesus this Christmas and let him come into our lives.

Narrator 1   We'll sing the song again and this time we'll add an extra verse and sing *Jesus* is knocking at the door.

11. Who's that knocking at the door? (reprise)

CD Track 11

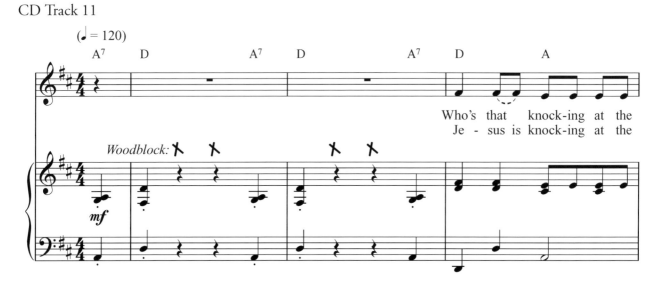

Narrator 2   Now we'll close our eyes and say a prayer.
Say after me –

Thank you God for Christmas. *(repeat)*
Thank you for sending Jesus to be with us. *(repeat)*
Thank you Jesus for knocking at our door *(repeat)*
and coming in to be our friend. *(repeat)*
Amen.

*Here would be a good place to thank and praise the children before standing
to sing the final carol.*

12. The Virgin Mary had a baby boy

CD Track 12

Words and Music: Traditional West Indian

See page 50 for an alternative song: 'See him lying on a bed of straw'

BLESSING
Now you've made your door, read on for more ideas . . .

Further Ideas

You have the door. What can you do with it?

Here are a few ideas and suggestions for other occasions.

Advent Sunday

Letters from the prophets

Either have a Postman carrying letters or have the characters come through the door themselves:

Isaiah – Unto us a child is born.

Micah – But you, Bethlehem . . .

John the Baptist – Prepare the way.

The Postman brings an invitation for everyone – are you ready? I'm coming soon. Who is it from?

Christmas Eve or Christmas Day

The Christmas Postman

Use the same basic material. This time make more of the Postman. He comes through the door with a letter from each character. The children can come through the door as before but just use the Knock! Knock! Who's there? for the Postman.

A letter from Mary: she wants to tell us what happened one day.

A letter from Joseph to Mary: 'Will you marry me?'

A letter from the Roman Governor: 'Go to your home town to be counted.'

A letter from Joseph: 'Can I book a room?' But oh dear, he forgets to post it.

A letter from Angel Gabriel to the rest of the angels: 'I'm going to see some shepherds tonight, so get ready to join me.'

A letter from the Wise Men to King Herod: 'We're trying to find a newborn King. Can you help us?'

A letter from Jesus to us: 'I'd love to come to your house.'

Another Nativity play

Use the same material but have different people coming as visitors at the beginning and use the alternative songs *(see pages 46-51)*.

When it isn't Christmas

There are many possibilities. Here are just a few suggestions:

A Who's Who? from the Old Testament – for example,
Joseph in his multicoloured coat

Moses (with a SatNav?)

David the shepherd-boy

David the king

Daniel

Jonah – with a ticket and a holiday brochure

A Who's Who from the New Testament – for example, the disciples

The disciples knock and come through the door – brothers could come together. They are interviewed by the service leader.

The Good Samaritan

The traveller comes through the door saying goodbye as he closes it. He sets off on his journey. Bandits creep through the door and follow the traveller. A priest comes through the door. A Levite comes through the door. The Samaritan comes through. He comes back to the door with the traveller and takes him in.

The Prodigal Son

Meet the characters through the door – the father, the elder son and the younger son.

The younger son waves goodbye. He comes to the door – it can be an inn or, if you're updating, a nightclub. He goes in. Position others behind the door and noises of a party in full swing.

Younger son comes out looking dejected – with no money.

He knocks at the door looking for work. He goes through – the noise of pigs grunting and squealing can be heard behind.

When he goes home, his father is standing at the door waiting for him.

And now, over to you!

Alternative
Songs

Mary, Mary, here comes an angel

Tune: 'Mary, Mary, quite contrary'

* or she'll

Joseph's song

Tune: 'London Bridge is falling down'

CD Track 14

1. We must go to Beth - le - hem, Beth - le - hem, Beth le - hem.
2. We must tra - vel all day long, all day long, all day long.
3. We must find a place to stay, place to stay, place to stay.

We must go to Beth - le - hem, my fair la - dy.
We must tra - vel all day long, my fair la - dy.
We must find a place to stay, my fair la - dy.

Shepherds in the fields one night

Tune: 'Polly, put the kettle on'

CD Track 15

Who is coming?

Tune: 'Frère Jacques'

CD Track 16

1. Who is com - ing? Who is com - ing? Three Wise Men, Three Wise Men.
2. Find the sta - ble, find the sta - ble, Three Wise Men, Three Wise Men.

Fol - low - ing the star - light, fol - low - ing the star - light to Beth - le - hem, Beth - le - hem.
See the ba - by Je - sus, see the ba - by Je - sus and wor - ship him, wor - ship him.

See him lying on a bed of straw

CD Track 17

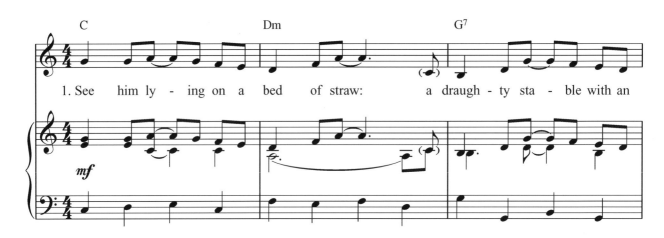

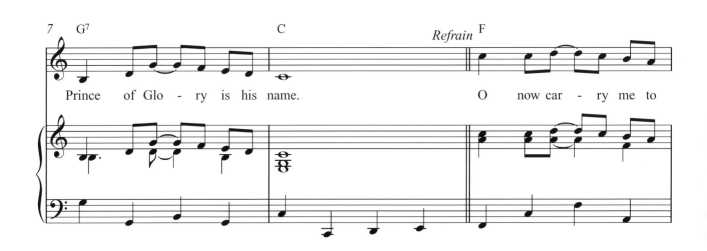

Beth - le - hem   to see the Lord   of love a - gain: just   as poor as was the

sta - ble then,   the Prince of Glo - ry when he came!

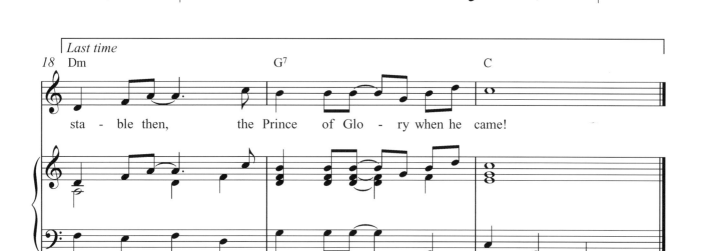

sta - ble then,   the Prince of Glo - ry when he came!

Words and Music: Michael Perry (1942-1996)
arr. Christopher Tambling

2. Star of silver, sweep across the skies,
   show where Jesus in the manger lies;
   shepherds, swiftly from your stupor rise
   to see the Saviour of the world!

3. Angels, sing again the song you sang,
   sing the glory of God's gracious plan;
   sing that Bethlehem's little baby can
   be the Saviour of us all.

4. Mine are riches, from your poverty;
   from your innocence, eternity;
   mine, forgiveness by your death for me,
   child of sorrow for my joy.

51

Song texts

1. O little town of Bethlehem

O little town of Bethlehem, how still we see thee lie!
Above thy deep and dreamless sleep the silent stars go by.
Yet in thy dark streets shineth the everlasting light;
the hopes and fears of all the years are met in thee tonight.

O morning stars, together proclaim the holy birth,
and praises sing to God the King, and peace to all the earth.
For Christ is born of Mary; and, gathered all above,
while mortals sleep, the angels keep their watch of wond'ring love;

How silently, how silently, the wondrous gift is giv'n!
So God imparts to human hearts the blessings of his heav'n.
No ear may hear his coming; but in this world of sin,
where meek souls will receive him, still the dear Christ enters in.

O holy child of Bethlehem, descend to us, we pray;
cast out our sin, and enter in, be born in us today.
We hear the Christmas angels the great glad tidings tell:
O come to us, abide with us, our Lord Emmanuel.

Phillips Brooks (1835-1893) alt.

2. Who's that knocking at the door?

Who's that knocking at the door?
Someone's knocking at the door.
Who can it be? Open it and see.
Who's that knocking at the door?

3. Mary, this is special news

Mary, this is special news,

special news, special news.

Mary, this is special news,

sent from God in heaven.

You will have a baby boy,

baby boy, baby boy.

You will have a baby boy,

sent from God in heaven.

Jesus is his special name,

special name, special name.

Jesus is his special name,

sent from God in heaven.

4. Little donkey

Little donkey, little donkey, on the dusty road,

got to keep on plodding onwards with your precious load.

Been a long time, little donkey, through the winter's night;

don't give up now, little donkey, Bethlehem's in sight.

Ring out those bells tonight, Bethlehem, Bethlehem,

follow that star tonight, Bethlehem, Bethlehem.

Little donkey, little donkey, had a heavy day,

little donkey, carry Mary safely on her way,

little donkey, carry Mary safely on her way.

Eric Boswell (1921-2009)

5. Twinkle, twinkle, special star

Twinkle, twinkle, special star,
how I wonder what you are.
Up above the world so high,
like a diamond in the sky.
Twinkle, twinkle, special star,
how I wonder what you are.

6. While shepherds watched their flocks

While shepherds watched their
     flocks by night,
all seated on the ground,
the angel of the Lord came down,
and glory shone around.

'Fear not,' said he,
(for mighty dread had seized
     their troubled mind)
'glad tidings of great joy I bring
to you and all mankind.

To you in David's town this day
is born of David's line
a Saviour, who is Christ the Lord;
and this shall be the sign:

The heav'nly babe you there
     shall find
to human view displayed,
all meanly wrapped in
     swathing bands,
and in a manger laid.'

Thus spake the seraph,
     and forthwith
appeared a shining throng
of angels praising God, who thus
addressed their joyful song:

'All glory be to God on high,
and on the earth be peace,
goodwill henceforth from
     heav'n to all
begin and never cease.'

Nahum Tate (1652-1715)

8.   Jesus is born in Bethlehem

You lift your left arm high, your right arm high,
left arm, right arm, wave them in the sky.
You clap your hands together and you turn around;
Jesus is born in Bethlehem.

Oh, glory alleluia.
Oh, glory alleluia.
Oh, glory alleluia.
Jesus is born in Bethlehem.

9.   Three Wise Men

Three Wise Men, three Wise Men
see a bright star, see a bright star.
Leading onward to Bethlehem,
shining there over Bethlehem;
follow the star up to Bethlehem,
three Wise Men.

10. Away in a manger

Away in a manger, no crib for a bed,
the little Lord Jesus laid down his sweet head.
The stars in the bright sky looked down where he lay,
the little Lord Jesus, asleep on the hay.

The cattle are lowing, the baby awakes,
but little Lord Jesus, no crying he makes.
I love thee, Lord Jesus! Look down from the sky,
and stay by my side until morning is nigh.

Be near me, Lord Jesus; I ask thee to stay
close by me for ever, and love me, I pray.
Bless all the dear children in thy tender care,
and fit us for heaven, to live with thee there.

William James Kirkpatrick (1838-1921)

11. Who's that knocking at the door?

Who's that knocking at the door?
Someone's knocking at the door.
Who can it be? Open it and see.
Who's that knocking at the door?

Jesus is knocking at the door.
Jesus is knocking at the door.
Open it and see. He's there for you and me.
Jesus is knocking at the door.

12. The Virgin Mary had a baby boy

The Virgin Mary had a baby boy,
the Virgin Mary had a baby boy,
the Virgin Mary had a baby boy,
and they say that his name was Jesus.

He come from the glory,
he come from the glorious kingdom,
he come from the glory,
he come from the glorious kingdom,
O yes, believer, O yes, believer,
he come from the glory,
he come from the glorious kingdom.

The angels sang when the baby born,
the angels sang when the baby born,
the angels sang when the baby born,
and proclaim him the baby Jesus.

Refrain

The wise men saw where the baby born,
the wise men saw where the baby born,
the wise men saw where the baby born,
and they say that his name was Jesus.

Refrain

Traditional West Indian

Song texts for alternative songs

Mary, Mary, here comes an angel

Mary, Mary, here comes an angel,
listen to what he'll (she'll) say.
'Now you will have a baby boy,
he'll be born on Christmas Day, he will,
he'll be born on Christmas Day.'

Mary, Mary, here comes an angel,
listen to what he'll (she'll) say.
'His name is Jesus, God's own Son,
he'll be born on Christmas Day, he will,
he'll be born on Christmas Day.'

Joseph's song

We must go to Bethlehem,
Bethlehem, Bethlehem.
We must go to Bethlehem,
my fair lady.

We must travel all day long,
all day long, all day long.
We must travel all day long,
my fair lady.

We must find a place to stay,
place to stay, place to stay.
We must find a place to stay,
my fair lady.

Shepherds in the fields one night

Shepherds in the fields one night
heard a voice and saw a light;
angels in the sky so bright
sang 'Peace on earth.'
You must go to Bethlehem,
there's a babe in Bethlehem;
find the stable, worship him,
sing 'Peace on earth.'

Who is coming?

Who is coming? Who is coming?
Three Wise Men, Three Wise Men.
Following the starlight,
following the starlight
to Bethlehem, Bethlehem.

Find the stable, find the stable,
Three Wise Men, Three Wise Men.
See the baby Jesus,
see the baby Jesus
and worship him, worship him.

See him lying on a bed of straw

See him lying on a bed of straw:
a draughty stable with an open door.
Mary cradling the babe she bore:
the Prince of Glory is his name.

O now carry me to Bethlehem
to see the Lord of love again:
just as poor as was the stable then,
the Prince of Glory when he came!

Star of silver, sweep across the skies,
show where Jesus in the manger lies;
shepherds, swiftly from your stupor rise
to see the Saviour of the world!

Refrain

Angels, sing again the song you sang,
sing the glory of God's gracious plan;
sing that Bethlehem's little baby can
be the Saviour of us all.

Refrain

Mine are riches, from your poverty;
from your innocence, eternity;
mine, forgiveness by your death for me,
child of sorrow for my joy.

Refrain

Michael Perry (1942-1996)

Please photocopy this page or visit our website for a downloadable version: www.kevinmayhew.com

KEVIN MAYHEW PERFORMANCE AND
PHOTOCOPYING LICENCE FORM

We are delighted that you are considering *Knock, knock! Who's there?* for production.
Please note that a performance licence is required and royalties are payable as follows:

10% of gross takings, plus VAT
***(Minimum fee: £22.00 + VAT = £26.40)**

This fee is valid until 31 December 2013.
After that date, please contact the Copyright Department for information.

This form should be returned to the Copyright Department at Kevin Mayhew Ltd.
A copy, including our performance licence number, will be returned to you.

Name of organisation _____

Contact name _____

Contact address _____

_____

Postcode _____

Contact telephone no. _____ Contact fax no. _____

Email _____

Date(s) of performance(s) _____

Venue _____

Seating capacity _____

*Proposed ticket price _____

Please tick:

☐   I am not charging admission for my performance.
     I enclose the minimum fee.

☐   I am charging admission and undertake to submit performance fees due to Kevin Mayhew Ltd
     within 28 days of the last performance, together with a statement of gross takings.

☐   I require a words-only photocopying licence and enclose £11.00 (inc. VAT).

Signature_____

Name (please print)_____

On behalf of _____

Address if different from above _____
- -
To be completed by Kevin Mayhew Copyright Department:

Performance/Photocopying Licence No. _____

is issued to _____ for _____ performance(s)

of _____ on _____

Signed _____ for Kevin Mayhew Ltd. Date _____

Copyright Department, Kevin Mayhew Ltd, Buxhall, Stowmarket, Suffolk, IP14 3BW
Telephone number: UK 01449 737978   International +44 1449 737978
Fax number: UK 01449 737834   International +44 1449 737834
Email: copyright@kevinmayhewltd.com